WORDS OF
Wisdom

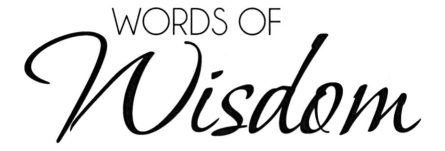

WORDS OF *Wisdom*

VOLUME 1

This is an inspirational book with Bible
references to guide our day-to-day life experience.

OYETUTU OSIBAJO

iUniverse LLC
Bloomington

WORDS OF WISDOM
Volume 1

iUniverse books may be ordered through booksellers or by contacting:

iUniverse LLC
1663 Liberty Drive
Bloomington, IN 47403
www.iuniverse.com
1-800-Authors (1-800-288-4677)

ISBN: 978-1-4759-9322-6 (sc)
ISBN: 978-1-4759-9323-3 (ebk)

Library of Congress Control Number: TXn1839522

Printed in the United States of America

iUniverse rev. date: 10/12/2013

Scripture quotations are from the Holy Bible, King James Version (KJV) of God's

Victorious Army Bible Copyright © 1996 and the Healing Bible copyright ©2000 by Morris Cerullo World Evangelism. Used by permission. New International

Version (NIV) ©1973, 1978, 1984 by International Bible Society. Used by permission. New American Standard Bible(NASB)®, copyright

©1960, 1962, 1963, 1968, 1972, 1973, 1975, 1977, 1995 by the Lock man Foundation. Used by permission.

For more information contact us: www.colem.org

Contents

Dedication

This book is dedicated to Dr. Morris Cerullo, on his eighty-first birthday; and the fiftieth anniversary of Morris Cerullo World Evangelism. You have been a great mentor and a father to me. God has used you to win souls for Christ all over the world.

I also send my appreciation to Mama Cerullo for all the support she has given and continues to give this great man of God. May God richly bless the two of you always as you continue to serve Him. We have learned a lot from you through the power of the Holy Spirit that dwells in you.

Acknowledgement

I thank the almighty God who gave me the insight and knowledge to write this book. I also thank the special people in my life who inspired me day and night to write it. They are: Mrs. Janet Oshinaja, Mrs. Helen Babalola and Mrs. Remi Awolowo. God Almighty will reward your support and encouragement.

And To my friend Mrs. Kendra Thimbrel, thank you for assisting me in the editing of my first edition. My special thanks goes to Professor Eunice Ajaiyeoba a retired professor who made further effort in editing this book. God sent you to me when I needed your wisdom the most. May you have unlimited success in all of your endeavors.

I especially recognize the support of my loving husband and daughters throughout the process of writing and compiling this book. I love you and I appreciate you. God will continue to bless and reward your endeavors. Thank you for the unwavering support and love.

Introduction

This book is a life changing book and it is an approach to finding solutions to different life issues. I know the importance of having the joy of getting out of valley or problems and working in the marvelous Joy of the Lord without sorrow.

Whatever you are going through now and whatever you have passed through I have the good news for you, this book will show how God can provide solutions to the issues that border you. It will also show you the different types of life situation and the words of wisdom that you can utilize for solutions.

This book was written by the inspiration of God and also from my experience, experiences of friends and family members. I know the Bible says we should seek wisdom, and those who have wisdom have understanding. This is the reason why this book was written to give us understanding on the ways to handle difficult life issues. The book envisages a time of difficulty and makes it known they are temporary and that we serve a God who never fails.

Words of Wisdom is meant to encourage you anytime an issue of life arises; given you the steps to take rather than allowing the situation to affect your health negatively through the followings health problems; For example sleepless night, frustration, unhappiness, hypertension and restlessness to mention a few. In addition this book shows how to find solutions to problems when needed, and taking advantages of opportunities that are opened to us through the wisdom of God.

I pray that God will bless you and help you in every life situation that may present itself in your life as you read this book.

How is your prayer life

The power of prayer is very important to us as children of God. We read in the Bible that prayer is the master key; Jesus started with prayer and ended with Prayer; through prayer we communicate with God. Prayer enables us to enter a new dimension with the Spirit of God. It is through prayer that our request can be known to God.

How is your prayer life? Do you pray regularly or pray only when you have problems? The Bible says in 1 Thessalonians 5:17(KJV) "Pray without ceasing." What does that mean? It means having the habit of praying in all occasions, at all times, for all things, and in every season. We read in Ephesians 6:18(NIV), "And pray in the Spirit, on all occasions with the kinds of prayers and request. With all this in mind, be alert and always keep on the praying for all the saints." The Bible also emphasizes in Romans 12:12(KJV), that we are to continue instantly in prayer.

As children of God, we need to know how to pray with power. We have to engage in prayers that are beyond the ordinary and charged by the Holy Spirit. God wants us to enter into the prayer that supersedes our natural mind and moves into the supernatural to take hold of the impossible, to demolish Satan's strongholds in our lives and our family. When praying, we must pray with boldness and with the power of His authority.

The words we use for our prayers have to be spoken with authority, and must be vested in the promises of God as the Spirit reveals to you.

While praying, we should bring ourselves into complete submission and yield to the Holy Spirit. This allows us to hear the audible voice of God speaking to us and giving us instructions and directions; through this, God will take us to a new dimension of power and authority in prayer. We must go deep into the realm of the Spirit, not only to bind the power over the enemy, but also to destroy his stronghold. The Bible says in Matthew 18:18(NIV), "I tell you the truth, whatever you bind on earth will be bound in heaven, and whatever you loose on earth is loose in heaven."

Prayer reveals to you the Spirit's powers and the root causes of the battles you are facing. Your battle is not against any sickness the enemy put on your body. Your battle is not with your husband, wife, child, family member, boss, fellow employee, financial condition, or overdue bills. According to Ephesians 6:12(KJV), "For we wrestle not against flesh and blood but against principalities, against powers, against the rulers of darkness of the world, against spiritual wickedness in high places." You should recognize that the battle is not physical but spiritual, and if you know your prayer life is weak, you need a change in your pray life.

We read in Romans 8:26(NIV), "In the same way, the Spirit helps us in our weakness. We do not know what we ought to pray for, but the Holy Spirit himself intercedes for us with groans that words cannot express." We need to allow the Holy Spirit to teach us how to pray, as we read in Luke 11:1 (KJV), "Lord, teach us to pray." When the Holy Spirit teaches you how to pray, your prayer will be pure, righteous, and full of the Spirit.

I encourage you to give yourself to prayer according to 1Corinthians 7:5(NIV): "Devote yourselves to prayer." This brings us to the type of prayer we can pray for different situations.

Forty types of prayer:

1. Prayer of confidence to face the enemy Psalm 3:18; 108:1-3; 27:1-4.
2. Prayer for mercy during trouble Psalm 136:1-26; 5:1-13; 36:1-12; 39:4-13.

3. Prayer for God to hear your cry and act Psalm 3:4; 10:1-18; 17:1-15; 80:1-19.
4. Prayer for deliverance Psalm 9:1-20; 31: 1-24; 116:1-19; 86:1-17; 120:1-7; 69:1-36; 70:1-5; 54:1-7.
5. Prayer of appeal for God's presence and keys to entering God's presence Psalm 15:1-5.
6. Prayer of praise Psalm 22:22-31; 48:1-14.
7. Prayer of thanksgiving Psalm 103:1-22; 111:1-10; 50:23;107:1-43; 149:1-9; 87:1-7; 52:9; 145:1-21; 92:1-15; 89:1-18;81: 1-16.
8. Prayer for guidance and protection Psalm 25:1-25; 23:1-6; 121:1-8; 125:1-5; 33:1-22; 140:1-13.
9. Prayer of forgiveness Psalm 51:1-19; 66:18.
10. Prayer to call upon God in distress Psalm 18:1-50; 143:1-12; 109:1-31; 86:7; 80:1-19; 56:1-13; 50:14-15; 39:4-13; 32:1.11.
11. Prayer for strength in fasting Psalm 27:14; 109:24; 69:10-11.
12. Prayer of a warrior Psalm 144:1-15; 35:1-28; 91:1-16; 18:1-50.
13. Prayer for salvation Psalm 119:145-152.
14. Prayer for comfort Psalm 119:81-88.
15. Prayer for peace Psalm 122:1-9; 119:161-168.
16. Prayer for understanding Psalm 119:169-176.
17. Prayer for the humble Psalm 131:1-3.
18. Prayer regarding oppression Psalm 12:1-8.
19. Prayer for promotion Psalm 75:1-10; 41:1-13; 37:34.
20. Prayer for restoration Psalm 147:1-20.
21. Prayer for proper conduct in the midst of trials Psalm 141:1.10.
22. Prayer of a troubled heart Psalm 61:1-8; 39:4-13.
23. Prayer for the victory power of God Psalm 76:1-12; 59:1-17; 59:1-17.
24. Prayer while waiting on the Lord Psalm 130:1-8; 27:4; 37:34.
25. Prayer in a time of betrayal Psalm 55:12-14; 41:9-10.
26. Prayer for the nations Psalm 67:1-7.
27. Prayer in the face of death Psalm 88:1-18.
28. Prayer of praise for God's deliverance and power Psalm 124:1-8.

29. Prayer to appeal for remembrance Psalm 132:1-18.
30. Prayer expressing trust in God Psalm 146:1-10.
31. Prayer of a believing heart Psalm 139:1-24.
32. Prayer while going through suffering Psalm 38:1:22; 74:1-23.
33. Prayer in obedience of God's command to seek Him Psalm27:8.
34. Prayer for fair judgment Psalm 26:12.
35. Prayer declaring the presence of God in times of calamity Psalm 46:1-11; 56:1-.13
36. Prayer for punishment of the wicked Psalm 58:1-11.
37. Prayer to plead for relief Psalm 74:1-23.
38. Prayer to praise the Creator and celebrate the greatness of God Psalm 29:1-4; 135:1-21.
39. Prayer for God's mercy Psalm 36:1-12; 85:1-13.
40. Prayer for God's blessings Psalm 30:1-12.

What can cure your worries?

Why are you worried? Why do you allow your heart to be filled with sorrow and anxiety? The Bible says in Mathews 6:25-34(NIV), Therefore, I tell you, do not worry about your life, what you will eat or drink: or about your body, what you will wear. Is not life more important than food, and the body more important than clothes? Look at the birds of the air: they do not sow or reap or store away in barns, and yet your heavenly father feeds them. Are you not much more valuable than they? Who of you by worrying can add a single hour to his life? Why do you worry saying, what shall we eat? Or what shall we drink? Or what shall we wear?

For your heavenly father knows that you need them. But seek first his kingdom and His righteousness, and all these things will be given to you as well. Therefore, do not worry about tomorrow, for tomorrow will worry about itself. Each day has enough trouble of its own. Why are you carrying the troubles of tomorrow through worries?

Real and imagined worries attack our minds daily. Pressures and stress on every side are an attempt to discourage and defeat us. But we have an assurance from the Bible in Mathew 6:30 that the Father knows before we ask. Jesus told us to seek above the filling of our needs, the release of blessings into our lives and answers to our problems through God's supernatural intervention on our behalf. When you do it this way, Jesus says, your needs will be filled according to His righteousness.

When you desire God's righteousness through Christ Jesus to be reflected in your words and actions, when you seek to execute His plan instead of your own plan, and when your primary goal is for the fulfillment of His kingdom within your heart and life, worry will cease to bind and control you. God will be freed to move to meet your needs.

Worries cannot solve your problem; instead, worries affect your health. And after the problem is solved, you are still battling with the health issue; which means you have allowed the problem to affect your health negatively through worries. Worries show sign of doubting God. Exhibiting the attitude of worrying brings no positive result. So why do you worry instead of putting your trust in God?

You should act as a child of God in order to allow the Holy Spirit the freedom to replace the worry that is keeping you awake night after night with the fullness of God and fullness of life of His kingdom. God wants you to be freed from those worries. He wants you to walk in financial freedom and in victory where there is no room for worries because you know God will supernaturally provide your needs. Have an attitude of releasing your faith instead of worrying.

Worries are signs that you have not relinquished your needs into God's hand. They also show that you are trying to work out your problems by yourself. As long as you are worried, you cannot go after your Father and ask in faith. Worries give birth to fear and doubt, and a doubtful person cannot receive from God (James: 6-7). They destroy health and affect the body physically and emotionally.

God is the author and finisher of your faith. He knows you more than you know yourself. Put your trust in Him, have faith in his works, walk with Him in holiness and truth, and take your request to him through prayer and fasting. Philippians 4:19(NIV), "And my God will supply all your needs according to His riches in Glory in Christ Jesus." Our Lord God can do more than you expect. As you walk your path, let God crown your effort. Do not worry.

He is able

What are your expectations? What are your desires? What have you been working on to receive from God? The good news is that God is able to accomplish your goals or desires much more than you expect. He is our God. He knows us more than we know ourselves and can see whatever we are going through or what we need. We read in 2Chronicles 25:9(KJV), "The Lord is able to give thee much more than this."

As a child of God, you have to exercise faith. Remember, faith is a fact, but faith is also an act. Faith does not come alive until you put it into action; and before you can move into action, you must exercise your will. Your faith makes you to expect what you need from God. The Bible says in Matthew 9:28(NIV) "When He had gone indoors, the blind men came to him, and he asked them, do you believe that I am able to do this? "Yes, Lord," they replied. Then he touched their eyes and said, "according to your faith will it be done to you"; and their sights were restored.

My question to you is, do you believe God is able to meet your needs? Your answer to this question will bring your miracle because you must be able to recognize the power and the authority in our Lord Jesus Christ and that nothing is impossible for Him to do for you. Through the exercise of faith, we have the same authority that is in our Lord Jesus Christ and with the power of the Holy Spirit that is flowing through us, we can see all our goals and heart's desires accomplished.

We only need to ask. The Bible says in Matthew 7:7-8(NASB), "Ask, and it shall be given you; seek, and you shall find; knock, and it shall be opened. For every one that asked received and to him that knocked it shall be open to you." God also promised us in John

14:14(NASB), "If you shall ask me anything in my name, I will do it." In the areas of your life where you are looking unto God, believe He is able to do abundantly and exceedingly.

God's giving to His children never stops. His giving is unlimited and goes far beyond what we can ever comprehend with our natural mind. He will do exceedingly and abundantly above all that we ask or think (Ephesians 3.20). The Bible says in Romans 4:20-21, "He staggers not at the promise of God through unbelief; but was strong in faith, giving glory to God. And being fully persuaded that, what he had promised, he was able to perform."

You have to look at God as your source of total supply, and never limit what God can do. The question before you today is this: will our mighty God, who gave us His only son, not freely give you all things? The answer is yes, He is able to give all things. You know what you want or what you are going through; now follow the steps to receive what you need from God.

Ways to receive from God:

- Ask God to forgive you in any areas you have limited Him.
- Have the will to receive from God (no matter how difficult it looks).
- Have a strong faith and trust in God that He is able. Never limit God's power in what He can do for you.
- Start praising and thanking Him for your heart's desires, even before you receive them.
- Sow a seed of faith toward your expectations.
- Recognize Him as the source of your total supply.
- Locate a word in the Bible that focuses on your area of need and quote it daily.
- Let your request be known to God with prayer and fasting.
- Allow peace in your mind and have a positive attitude.

I join my faith with you, and I pray that God will answer all your heart's desires according to His will for you, amen.

See yourself as blessed

It is common to hear people speak about the riches of others and about themselves as being poor using their usual words, "I am managing." Do you know that we are blessed in different ways by God? Some blessings are visible and some are invisible.

Visible blessings can be categorized as riches and wealth through business, job, sport, and music, to mention a few. Invisible blessings are your ideas, the creative works of your hand, your talents, and unseen opportunities. A lot of people look at themselves as poor and praise others with riches instead of working at recognizing their personal talents.

The Bible says in Mathews 25:14-15(NASB), "For it is just like a man about to go on a journey, who called his individual slaves and entrusted his possession to them, to one he gave five talents to another, two, and to another one, each according to his ability, and he went on his journey." However, in this passage we found out that some used their talents, some started and stop on the way, and some never used or even touched their talents.

My question is, which group do you belong to in the above story? Check yourself and find the ideas in you that you have not utilized and tell me if you are not blessed. Use the time you spend on speaking against yourself and praising the wealthy people to detect your potentials. It is never too late to start. The end justifies the means. Therefore, brainstorm on your talents, interests and hobbies you liked as a child and as an adult. You could activate your talents by starting somewhere with the financial resources you have or look for divine helpers who believe in your ideas. You also have to include God in your endeavors, allowing Him to direct your steps. When you use your talents and involve God in your life, the result is God's abundant blessings.

Do not condemn yourself

Are you condemning yourself for your past actions or allowing others to condemn you? If you forsake your past sinful ways and you are doing God's will sincerely, I have a good news for you. The Bible says in Romans 8:1(NASB), "Therefore, there is now no condemnation for those who are in Christ Jesus." Why do you still condemn yourself when you have been set free? As we read in Romans 8:2(NASB) "For the law of the spirit of life in Christ Jesus has set you free from the law of sin and of death." Do not put your mind on those things that are flesh, but let the Spirit of God lead you. I want to encourage you that God does not judge the way we judge. He looks at the heart and qualifies the unqualified.

If we look at some biblical examples, we see that those we condemned for sinful actions against God were those God forgave and used to do exploit for Him. For example, Jacob cheated and lied; Noah was a drunkard; Saul, whose name was changed to Paul, murdered people; Elijah was depressed; Thomas doubted; David was involved in adultery; Abraham and Sarah were impatient; and Jonah disobeyed God. There is a saying that God does not think the way human beings think. Stop condemning yourself and get yourself ready to do His will so God can use you.

God was called the God of Jacob in Psalm 46:7 (NIV), "The Lord Almighty is with us the God of Jacob is our fortress" to show you how merciful God is to us. After all Jacob did, God did not condemn him. Jacob did not condemn himself; when he had the opportunity, he wrestled with the angel to change his life. Jacob's name was changed to Israel to show God's compassion on him and also signify a change to a new and righteous life. When Jacob's name was changed he left his old ways of life to live a God fearing life (Genesis 32:22-31). Are you as determined to change as Jacob was? All you need is to repent from your old ways and live a holy and righteous life.

The first step Jacob took was to acknowledge God by asking God to be with him and promising to do God's will (Genesis 28:20-22). Are you willing to surrender yourself and confess your sin to Him? Are you willing to get out of self-condemnations and look up to God who forgives? Say these words: God, I repent of my sin and I invite you to be my Lord and Savior. Forgive my sins and have mercy on me. Renew a right spirit within me, and "show me your ways that give salvation."

Life is what you make it

Those who are wise make haste while the sun shines, which means they make use of every opportunity they encounter. An undisciplined man or woman plays and jokes around. They procrastinate and fail to take action at the right time. Life is what you make of it. If you see it positively, things around you will be much better. There might be challenges, but your positive thinking in handling those problems does not allow challenges to rule your life. Instead, it allows you to rule over those challenges by applying wisdom, patience, endurance, and faith with works, seeking new ideas to solve problems and also seeking God's help through prayers.

When you view life negatively, there is really a problem. No matter whatever people do to help and encourage you, you are blind to their observations and assistance, because you cannot see beyond your imagination. Since you are rigid and cannot accept others' opinions, you can't change. You must realize that this kind of attitude cannot bring positive results. It makes you see others' blessings and ignore the good ones in you. It makes you a complainer and a jealous, hateful, and wicked person.

Why are you jealous and hateful? You have allowed frustration and condemnation in yourself. You need to invite God to help you, and become fulfilled as you see things positively instead of negatively. You need to change your attitude, recognize opportunities and use them wisely.

How to deal with disobedient children

The Bible says, "Lo, children are the heritage of the Lord and the fruit of the womb is his reward." Psalms 127:3 (KJV) "But Jesus called unto him, and said, Suffer little children to come unto me; and forbid them not, for of such is the kingdom of God" (Luke 18:16 KJV). Isaiah said, "Behold, I and the children whom the Lord has given me, are for signs and for wonders" (Isaiah 8:18 NASB). God's promise for us is that our children will walk as children of light. We read in Ephesians 5:8 (NIV) "Live as children of light." God gave us our children that they will be children of God by faith in Christ (Galatians 3:26).

There is a continuation of God's promises over our children. In 3 John 3:4, God said our children will walk in truth. God also said our children will be called blessed, as the Bible says, "He hath blessed thy children within thee" (Psalm 147:13 KJV).

This brings me to the questions on how you train your children. Do you train them to have the fear of God? Do you show them the right way of life, or do you allow them to follow the ways of ungodly life, character, and behavior that you exhibit in their presence? Do you correct them with love when they are wrong or chastise them with nagging or a negative attitude? We have to realize that children are prompt to copy or follow bad examples without thinking. They see all we do, and when they put it in practice, we call it disobedience. If a child behaves in a certain way, check the behavior of both parents. A child with bad temper has a parent acting in the same way.

If you behaved badly when you were young and observe that character even more in your children, go back to God and ask for forgiveness, and ask God to change your children. The Bible says, "One that rules well his own house, having his children in subjection with all gravity" (1Timothy 3:4KJV). How do you deal with issues on disobedient children in your home? What parenting skills do you use to deal with disobedient children? Are you showing them good or bad examples? The Bible says in Proverbs 17:16, "The glory of the children, are in their father."

What conduct have you subjected your children to in which they are now experts? Are you a parent who lies in front of children or drinks excessively? Have you fornicated or stolen with the kind of business you operate, or are you malicious, backbiting, or jealous? Do you have hatred or act disrespectfully, Do you always want your way and disobey laws? Children watch all these, and when they practice them, you call it disobedience; this is not disobedience. The children are exhibiting your bad behaviors. Their behaviors are the fruits of your actions in their presence Change has to start from the home and your actions while your children are present. We need to live uprightly for the children to see a change and for them to have a brand-new character.

Methods for changing disobedience in children:

- Speak to them with love.
- Let them know the consequence of disobedience according to the Bible.
- Pray with them and teach them the ways of the Lord.
- Create time to talk with your children to know what they are going through.
- No matter how their behavior is, do not condemn them but encourage them in the Lord.
- Help them by encouraging them and showing them good examples.
- Abstain from negative behavior in the presence of children.
- Control your anger and do not nag your children. Give peace a chance, and believe God for a change.

Are you a parent who has lived a godly life, yet your children have developed an attitude of disobedience? You have to take positive steps and ask God for help. The Bible recognized this in Isaiah 1:2(KJV), "Hear, O heaven, and give ear, O earth: for the Lord hath spoken, I have nourished and brought up children, and they have rebelled against me." So, pray for them and find out what kind of friends they have. Monitor the programs your child watches on the television. Show them **unconditional love;** don't embarrass them in front of their friends or family. Remember their special days, for example birthdays by doing special things with them.

Have special days with your child, take them out. While your child is in a good mood, start advising him or her, speak about the fear of God and how God hates disobedience. The Bible says in Ephesians 5:6(KJV), "Let no man deceive you with vain words: for because of these things cometh the wrath of God upon the children of disobedience." Emphasize to your child the result of disobedience before God and how God said not to partake with those who do evil.

Create a strong relationship with your child by inviting him or her to pray with you and share the word of God together. You must create time for your child in your schedule; agree with your child on a convenient time that suits both of you. Make sure he or she is in a peaceful environment that has a positive influence. Do not be upset because of the bad conduct. If your child is still disobedient after talking about it, allow room for change, and continuously demonstrate love.

If you need tolerance, ask God as a parent. Refer your child to Bible passages such as 1 John 5:2(KJV)" By this we know that we love the children of God, when we love God, and keep his commandments. Let your children know that you love the children of God.

As a parent, encourage your children that they are children of God and that you love them. I pray that God will remove the disobedience out of your children and make them children of the highest (Luke 6:35), children of promise (Romans 9:8), Children that are taught peace (Isaiah 54:13). Lord, let our attitude and conduct be godly, that our children would call us blessed (Proverbs 31:28). God bless our children and protects them from all evil and unfriendly friends. Give them the heart to love and fear God. Amen

Is your marriage in a valley?

What is marriage? It is the union of a man and a woman. According to Ephesians 5:31 (NASB), "For this reason a man shall leave his father and mother and shall be joined with his wife, and the two shall become one flesh." Marriage should be a union of love and understanding between spouses and backed up with the fear of God.

What kind of marriage do you have? Is it the Godly one in which there is peace and harmony within the home, with obedience and respectful children? If you are in this group, I congratulate you and thank God on your behalf. For those who are in a valley situation in their marriage, I pray God will deliver you and give you peace.

What do we mean by marriage in a valley? These are marriages in which there is no peace, no joy and no focus. There are arguments and fighting, competition instead of unity. The home has become a battle field and a boxing ring. The spouses are not on the same terms and everyone is on different directions doing their own things. For example, one may be doing God's will while the other is not. A valley does not give rest in the marriage. It means going from one problem to another.

People always believe the liar when two spouses are in a valley. Because of that person's deceitful innocent look and satanic wisdom, he or she makes the honest, suffering spouse look bad when they have issues. Why? The innocent ones become bitter, angry, frustrated, depressed, lost trust, and felt betrayed in the valley experience they are going through. They cannot express themselves or know what to say when asked questions because of the shock experience from the lying spouse and the unfair mediator.

Some spouses use marriage to cheat and steal from each other. Some caused health problems to themselves through the disappointment they encounter in the marriage. Some become depressed and some are yet to recover from the amazement of the treatment they received from their spouse. We should not allow our bitter experience from our marriage create negative health issues for us. We should find ways to identify the problems and find godly ways to solve them.

What causes valley experiences?

- A spouse who does not encourage but always belittle his or her partner.
- A disrespectful and arrogant spouse
- A spouse who argues, quarrels, and fights
- A stingy, selfish, and self-centered spouse
- A spouse who discuss issues of the family to people and as a result create enmity for the other spouse
- Children who live ungodly lives and frustrate all the efforts of their parents to help them
- A spouse who became ungrateful and went after another person.
- A marriage that is unfulfilled and discouraging because of the conduct of both spouses
- A marriage with financial problems and difficulties in meeting marital responsibilities.
- Problems with in-laws
- Health issues that made a spouse change and act strangely
- Lack of Children in the family, which causes indifference in the marriage or the preference of having a particular sex. (In some cultures they prefer male children over female children)

I have good news for you. God can turn things around for you if you believe. The Bible says in Psalm 68.19, "Blessed is the Lord, who daily bears our burden." Whatever you are going through in the valley, God knows about it, and you are not alone in the problem, God Almighty is with you and He will stand by you to give you victory. According to 1Peter 5:7(NIV) "Cast all your anxiety on Him for He cares for you." The valley is temporary if you trust God and have strong faith that you can do all things through Christ who strengthens you.

Ways to get out of a valley:

- As a family, acknowledge God in your home.
- Have the fear of God in your relationship.
- Have the love of God (*agape* love).
- Have respect for each other.
- Pray together and share the Word as a family.
- Ask God for direction in your marriage.
- Avoid selfishness and covetousness among you.
- Correct yourself from bad habits, and recognize your weakness that affect the other party.
- Ask God for wisdom to deal with a difficult spouse.
- Pray for each other's weaknesses during your personal prayer time.
- Have the interest of your family in mind. Do not be like those who help others but ignore their family.
- Do not share your family problems with people who will misled you.
- Encourage each other and respect each other's feelings and opinions.
- Do not involve a third party to dictate the affairs of your marriage.(In-law and friends)
- Honestly write what you dislike in each other and meditate on it for a positive change.

- Correct each other with love, and have a spirit of forgiveness.
- Remind God to fulfill what you need in your marriage according to His will, and serve God as a family.

As you do these things, God Almighty will bring peace and the joy of the Lord to your marriage and family. Please say this after me: My marriage and I have been set free from the valley. Amen.

God's supernatural provision

How can we achieve a financial breakthrough and God's supernatural provision? As children of God, we know and believe that God is the source of our supply. His promise for us is to supply our needs according to His riches in glory through Christ Jesus. Christ gave it all for our sake that we might become wealthy. This was not compulsory; He gave His vast, immeasurable wealth and riches willingly so that you and I can no longer be poor.

The world thinks of poverty as not having the earth's wealth and riches. Those who are considered rich are those who have accumulated great wealth and an abundance of possessions. In the kingdom of God, those who are rich are people like the apostle Paul, who have learned to look to God for his supernatural provision. As a child of God, if you set your affection on things above and on the work of the Lord, though you may have little of the world's goods and be poor according to the world's standards, you will be rich, having the access to all that God possesses.

The good news for you is that Christ took your poverty spiritually, physically, materially upon Himself and carried it to the cross. He did not pay the supreme sacrifice for your sins alone, but for all your needs including your physical and financial needs. You have a covenant relationship with God that you are rich and will achieve your purpose in life. You will have all that you need and more because you have been made a joint heir; you are not limited by the prosperity and riches of the world. You have direct access to the Father and all that He has, belong to you. You do not need to rely on your own limited resources. You have access to the resources of heaven! You have unlimited access to all that the Father has, and you can go directly to Him and draw all that you need through your covenant relationship with God which Christ made possible.

As a child of God, you have provision for all your needs—salvation, health, peace, protection, security, prosperity, and deliverance. Through your covenant with Him, there is divine sufficiency, abundance, without any lack.

Do not doubt God's supernatural provision for your life. Trust Him, do His will, and obey His words to enter the covenant that bring provision. Do not allow your financial needs and limited resources affect your focus on God. Lay your problems at the feet of Jesus Christ walk in the covenant with God in whom you draw your needs. Attack your financial circumstances with new strength knowing that God will not withhold anything from you, as you come to Him in faith. The Bible says in Psalm 84:11(KJV), ". . . . No good thing will He withhold from those who walk uprightly." When you honor God and focus on him, He will not withhold good things from you. He will make continuous supernatural provisions for you.

Ways to receive God's Supernatural Provision

- Walk uprightly with God.
- Increase the fruit of your righteousness.
- Give thanks to God.
- Know God's purpose for your life.
- Pray for a breakthrough in understanding, and fulfilling His promises in your circumstances.
- Love and support the work of God.
- Ask for a fresh revelation of God's plan and provision for your life.
- Have a personal relationship with God.
- Faithfully walk in obedience to God.
- Surrender your problems to Jesus Christ.

We read in 2 Corinthians 9:10-12 (NIV), "Now He who supplies seed to the sower and bread for food will also supply and increase your store of seed and enlarge the harvest of your righteousness.

You will become rich in all your ways so that you can be a blessing to others. Your generosity will result in thanksgiving to God because of the people you have helped with your blessings. This service that you provide is not only supplying the needs of God's people but it is also overflowing in many expressions of thanks to God."

In these verses, there are five powerful keys for walking in financial victory and living God's promises of supernatural provision:

1. God will provide seed for you to sow.
2. God will supply your needs.
3. God will increase your seed.
4. There will be continual supply.
5. God will increase the harvest of your righteousness.

When you move in God's direction for your life, all His promises to give you His supernatural provisions will come to pass. I pray that my God will supply all your needs according to His riches in Glory through Christ Jesus, and you will continue to dwell in abundance. Amen.

The gift of excellence and understanding

We often see people struggling with their careers, education, license examinations, and decision making. As children of God, we need to ask God for the gift of excellence and understanding so we can succeed in all our endeavors. In Colossians 1:9(KJV), the Bible says, "For this cause, we also, since the day we heard it, do not cease to pray for you, and to desire that you might be filled with the Knowledge of His will in all wisdom and spiritual understanding." It is when you pray for it that you receive it. The Bible says, "For as much as an excellent spirit and knowledge and understanding interpreting dreams, Daniel was preferred above the president and princes because excellent spirit was in him" (Daniel 5:12; 6:3). Be determined that you need this gift from God so that you can be distinguished from your associates.

However, there are criterions for getting the gift. The Bible says in 1 Corinthians 14:12(NIV), "So it is with you. Since you are eager to have the spiritual gift, try to excel in gift that builds up the church." This means you must serve God by praying, praising, speaking in tongues, and winning souls for God. As you involve yourself in the aforementioned practices, God will give you the gifts that will help other areas of your life. For example, spiritually growth, physical growth, emotional growth. Your new growth will have impact on your education, job, and how you make yourself available to your family, friends and community. We excel only because of the glory of God in our life (2Corinthians 3:10). For us to be excel in life, it has to come from God. God is the source of our greatness in life. When you request a spirit of excellence, and you focus on God, live a righteous life, He will give you wisdom, understanding and the spirits of excellence.

The Bible says that the advantage of knowledge is this: wisdom lengthens the life of its possessor. God helps you distinguish between good and bad, holiness and evil ways. When you follow the right path to excellence, you have long life. You have to stop counting on your own strength and understanding just surrender all to God. Let Him direct the affairs of your life and lift you up. If you need success in your career and the affairs of your family, God will impact you with the spirit of excellence and wisdom. The Bible says, ". . . . I will make you an external excellency, a joy of many generations" (Isaiah 60:15 KJV).

I pray that you excel in any area where you have been struggling in life physically, financially, or emotionally. The gift of excellence will be given to you to provide the solution to your need in Jesus' name.

Do you rejoice with others?

How do you feel when others are giving testimonies or reporting the goodness of God in their lives? Do you respond with joy from your heart or do you envy them? Do you use it as an open door for your blessing, or do you use it to pass rumors around about them because of jealousy. Examine your heart and character in the ways you react, and be sincere with your findings.

It is wise, when you witness or hear about the accomplishment of others; use the achievement as a point of contact for your situation. It is surprising to see some wealthy people humiliate the less privileged ones because of their wealth. Blessing is not apportioned for a particular group of people. Blessing is for those who can tap into it. According to Philippians 4:19(NASB), "And my God will supply your needs according to his riches in glory in Christ Jesus." When you are blessed, God wants you to use it to bless others. In addition God wants you to be happy for those who are blessed like you.

We need to change our attitude. The Bible says in John 14:28(KJV), ". . . If you love me; you will rejoice . . ." When you encounter your family, friends, colleagues, church members, and neighbors excel in their endeavors, rejoice with them as a child of God. We read in Deuteronomy 26:11(KJV), "And thou shall rejoice in every good thing which the Lord; thy God has given unto thee . . . ." This means rejoicing in the accomplishment of others is an open door for God to rejoice over you.

If you are still waiting for God's rejoicing and your associates are experiencing great achievement, do not be angry and detestable.

The Bible says in Proverbs 31:25(KJV), "And she shall rejoice in time to come."

Remember that God has not forgotten you, and your time of rejoicing will soon come. Rejoice now, with those who are rejoicing. God Almighty will help us to sincerely rejoice with those who are rejoicing.

Who are your friends?

Who are your friends and how have they influenced your life? God loves us so much that He gave us His son for the remission of our sins and for us to have salvation. God influenced our lives by taking us out of sin and giving us abundant life.

Do you have human beings as your only friend, or do you choose God as your Father and best friend? In the book of Genesis, God called Abraham a friend of God. Why? He was obedient and sincere in serving God.

Are you obedient to, God or Man? Some have friends who make decisions on what they should do. We should be like our father Abraham who had a personal relationship with God (Genesis 17:1-3) and constantly depend on God's directions. As a result of this association with Abraham, God made a covenant with Abraham, and his generation. There are other people who had intimate relationship with God as Abraham did.

For example David made God his father and friend; he developed a personal relationship with God by praising Him always and seeking for His direction before making any decision. God made a covenant with David (2 Samuel 7: 8-17). When David walked in sin, he did not go to men but to God for forgiveness (Psalm 51:1-19).

Additionally, Moses was called by God and had a personal relationship with Him (Exodus 3:1-22). Subsequently, Moses wrote the Ten Commandments (Exodus 20:1-18) through the personal relationship which he had with God.

All these men decided to have a personal relationship with God rather than men. As a result they were always guided by the Holy Spirit.

Do your friends do any of the following?

- Gossip and secretive?
- Steal and untrustworthy?
- Kill spiritually and physically with comments and actions?
- Hate others for no reason?
- Backbite and filled with wickedness?
- Envious?
- Have no Knowledge about God but in worldly affairs.
- Arrogant?
- Disobedient and rebellious?
- Faithless and discouraging?
- Manipulative?
- Selfish and continuously demand your help?
- Love you for materials things?

The good news is that those who choose God to be their friend and Father have all these attributes from God: humility, love, fear of God, peace of mind, obedience, trust, blessings, forgiveness, uprightness, and the fullness of God's grace.

Here are some of the qualities of a Godly friend:

- The fear of God
- Honesty and not secretive
- Not controlling
- Not envious
- Speaks and acts in Godly ways
- Does not seek to destroy others
- Have strong faith in God
- Encouraging and helpful

- Speaks peace always and rejoices in your achievements
- A good motivator and not a manipulator.

I pray you choose God as your friend to direct and guide you in every area of your life. He is the only friend you can count on and He will never disappoint you.

Pride goes before destruction

What is pride? It is inordinate self-esteem or disdainful behavior and a delight arising from some act, possession, or relationship. "Pride comes from the heart and defiles the man (Mark 7:22-23 (KJV)." Why are you proud when the Bible says that the fear of the Lord is to hate evil, pride, arrogance, and the evil way, and the forward mouth, do I hate? (Proverbs 8:13 (KJV) this means that if you are proud, you have no fear of God because those who fear God have no pride in them but humility. The Bible says in Proverbs 11:2(NIV), "When pride comes, then come disgrace, but with humility comes wisdom."

What makes you proud and conceded? Is it because of your riches, your knowledge, your accomplishments, or your looks, to mention a few? All these things are vanity. When you die, all hope perishes; all you expected from your power and riches come to nothing. We read in Proverbs 16:18(NIV), "Pride goes before destruction, a haughty spirit before a fall." The Bible says in Proverbs 29:23(KJV) "A man's pride brings him low: but honor shall uphold the humble in spirit." When a mind is hardened in pride, it can cause ones glory to be lost. We read in Daniel 5:20 (NIV), "But when his heart became arrogant and hardened with pride, he was deposed from his royal throne and stripped of his glory."

Here is a word of wisdom: when you are proud, people have no respect for you but the respect if there is any at all is on what they can get from you. Also, people are not interested in helping or preventing you from destruction because of your pride. For example, if a proud person makes a mistake, all attentions are on Him and the mistake. However, if a humble person makes the same mistake, people will overlook it because they respect him. Humility makes people love you, and pride attracts enemies to work on reducing the achievement of the proud person and force him to be humble.

The Bible says in Ezekiel 16:49(NIV), "Now this was the sin of your sister Sodom. She and the daughters were arrogant, overfed and unconcerned: they did not help the poor and needy. They were haughty and did detestable things before me. Therefore, I did away with them as you have seen." When you are proud and stubborn, God says He will displace you and put you aside as He did for King Nebuchadnezzar. If the most arrogant person in the Bible can say in Daniel 4:37(NIV), "Now I, Nebuchadnezzar, praise and exalt and glorify the King of heaven, because everything he does is right and all his ways are just, And those who walk in pride, He is able to humble," why are you going to wait for God to humble you by force?

There is room for change. Pray and ask God to forgive you of your pride, and humble yourself with What God gave you. Acknowledge Him with your riches, help the poor, the needy, and the ministries of God, and His peace will abide with you.

What is faith?

"Faith is the substance of things hoped for, the evidence of things not seen" (Hebrews 11:1). As a child of God, you must always walk in faith, not by sight. You need to break out of the way you perceive things in your environment with your natural eyes and enter a rhythm of miracles where your spiritual eyes are governed by faith which is God's miracle power through which all things are possible.

Faith makes you believe in the midst of the obstacles or circumstance you are going through that seem hopeless. The spiritual eyes of faith is a means to show that solutions will come through our Lord Jesus Christ by prayer, fasting, reading His words, avoiding sin, and believing Him. With faith, no matter what Satan has placed in your way to defeat you, you will not be discouraged and hopeless. Instead, by faith and with your spiritual eyes, you will be able to see God supernaturally intervene in your circumstances. You will live in daily expectancy of the miracle of God.

A life of faith is a life full of expectations. God tells us to expect to receive from Him because He rewards those that diligently seek Him, and it is impossible to please him without faith. We read in Hebrew 11:6 (NIV), "And without faith it is impossible to please God, because anyone who come to him must believe that he exists and that He rewards those who earnestly seek him." Faith makes you believe, you will experience God's grace. Some of them are peace, debts settled, happiness over your children, good marriage, good health, better career, promotion, and financial increase, to mention a few.

Faith in Him will change your thought, emotions, speech, sight, and hearing. Faith also brings them under the influence and control of the Holy Spirit. When you have faith you will never be moved by any circumstances.

You will always speak positively to situations and have faith like a mustard seed that everything is under God's control, every situation will turn around to be wonderful and glorious in the name of Jesus Christ. Faith requires you put your believe into action; therefore, follow your plan for every situation you are believing God for by reading your bible daily, seeking God's help through prayer, have unshakeable faith, fast and do God's will, for God to crown your effort with success.

Standing in faith

"Now Faith is the substance of things hoped for, the evidence of things not seen" (Hebrews 11: 1 KJV). To stand in faith means to focus on your hope without allowing distractions that may occur on the way. Standing in faith makes you tear down the barriers of unbelief. Every time they try to distract you and hold you back, you stand on the positive force of God's Word. When you face a decision either to listen to the voice of negativity, or unbelief, or to listen to the voice of God as He speaks to you through Word, you must set your will, and determine in your heart that you are going to obey the voice of God, regardless of what you hear, feel, or think. This is called standing in faith.

Standing in faith also means you allow the Holy Sprint to do His work; there is no end as to how God can transform you. Standing in faith means taking your rightful position as a true son or daughter of the living God; knowing that He will give you strength and courage to face every circumstance; every fiery dart of the enemy without fear and knowing that God has already given you victory. For example, consider people who stood in faith and received victory in the Bible such as Shadrach, Meshach, and Abed-nego when the king ordered that they be cast in the furnace of blazing fire (Daniel3:16-26).

Other examples in the bible are Daniel, when he was put in the lion's den (Daniel 6:16-26); and Paul and Silas, while imprisoned prayed and praised the Lord, and suddenly there was a great earthquake and they got their victory. As children of God, we need to stand in faith and trust in the Lord we serve.

When you have faith and focus on God by reading His Word daily, praying, praising God, fasting, and living a holy and righteous life, you are standing in faith and He will always be there for you as He was for Daniel and others in the Bible.

Faith and works

The Bible says in James 2:14 (NASB), "What use is it, my Brethren, if someone says he has faith but has no works? Can that faith save him? If a brother or sister is without clothing and in need of daily food, and one of you says to them, "Go in peace, be warmed and filled," and yet you did not give them what is necessary for their body, what use is that? Even so faith, if it has no works, is dead, being by itself. But someone may well say, you have faith and I have works, show me your faith without the works, and I will show you my faith by my works."

You should recognize as a child of God that faith without works is useless, According to Romans 5:1 (NASB) "Therefore Being justified by faith, we have peace with God through Jesus Christ." Our father Abraham was justified by faith, when he was to offer Isaac, his son, on the altar. You see that faith was working with his works, and as a result of the works, faith was perfected and Scripture was fulfilled.

A man is justified by works and not by faith alone. This means as a child of God who has faith, you must justify your faith by action to make it work. If you are jobless, sick, have financial problems, or are frustrated due to other issues, you have to justify your faith with works by applying for different jobs or start your own business, having the mind that you will recover from the sickness and employed; and you must work hard towards achieving your goals.

You can also take a Godly action to stop what is causing your frustration by asking God to give you peace of mind while fulfilling your obligations on how to make faith works. For examples, if you have financial problem work on how to have financial breakthrough and monitor your spending. If you are sick have faith that you are healed, don't say anything negative about your sickness. Thank God in advance that you are healed.

If you are in need and you know who can help you, but they cannot see your needs, ask for help. There is a saying that heaven helps those who help themselves. The Bible says for just as body without spirit is dead, so also faith without works is dead James 2: 20 (NASB) Now, faith is the substance of things hoped for, the evidence of things not seen.

Faith without work is useless. If you have faith that you can achieve your heart's desires, you need to take necessary actions to get it because you have faith. Faith and works bring success. Faith without works brings disappointment. To achieve your goals, you need to work hard and have faith.

I pray that you keep your faith alive with works to get your blessings.

The time to change

When God's appointed time to change your situation comes, it will look like a miracle, and this happens in a second. God can change a situation that look as if it will never end. In the Bible, we read about how God changed the circumstances of the following people:

- God changed the life of Sarah at the age of ninety (Genesis21:1-2).
- God changed the life of Jacob and also changed his name to Israel (Genesis 28:10-22).
- God changed the life of Hannah in Shiloh when God gave her a son called Samuel (1Samuel 1:12-20).
- God changed the life of Naaman when Elisha instructed him to and dip himself seven times in River Jordan; the leprosy left him. (2 king 5:14 (NASB) "So he went down and dipped himself seven times in River Jordan, according to the words of the man of God; and his skin was restored like the skin of a baby and he was cleaned from leprosy"
- God changed the life of Obededom the Gittite when David took the ark of God to his house, and this brought the blessings of God to his entire household in three months (1 Chronicles 13:13-14).
- God changed Esther an orphan with little beginning to a queen because of the grace and favor of God (Esther2:17).
- God changed Mordecai from a gate man to second in command (Esther 8:1-2).
- God changed the life of Joseph from a prisoner to second in command. God also empowered him with spirit of interpretation that took him to a higher level. (Genesis 41:40-41) (NASB) "You shall be over my entire house and according to your command all my people shall do

homage; only in the throne I will be greater than you. Pharaoh said to Joseph, "See I have set you over the land of Egypt."
- God changed the life of Saul and also changed his name to Paul and made him a great apostle (Act 9:1-18).
- God changed the life of Jabez when he called on God to bless him. (1 Chronicles 4:10 (NASB) "Now Jabez called on the God of Israel, saying, "Oh that you would bless me indeed and enlarge my border, and that your hand might be with me . . . ."

Our Lord Jesus Christ brought us change when he died on the cross to give us salvation. Change can occur in different ways:

- Heart (pouring out your soul and mind to the Lord)
- Words of our mouth (positive words)
- Dreams
- Vision
- Praising God
- Obedience
- Faith

How do you know there is a change?

- It is visible
- It leads to joy.
- It brings peace of mind.
- It shows in your attitude.
- It leads to praising God.
- Your life is never the same.

I don't know what you are expecting from God, but I want to give you the good news that the God who changed the life of the above-mentioned people is still the same God. He has never changed, and He will surely change your situation for better. And the joy of the Lord will be in your home, life, job, marriage, children, health, business, and all your endeavors in Jesus name.

The Favor of God

The Bible says in 1Samuel 2:26 (KJV), "And the child Samuel grew on, and was in favor both with the Lord; and also with men." As a child of God who has faith in Him, no matter what you are going through, God Almighty will send favor. Favor is not what you merit, but a great blessing from God. It is God's desire, to favor His children. When divine favor is released by God upon your life, it blesses you beyond your imagination. People will compete among themselves to bestow favor upon you, simply because you have found favor with God.

Our Lord has promised to favor us in many ways. And when the time comes, as the Bible says in Psalm 102:13, "He will arise and have compassion on Zion, for it is time to favor her; the appointment time has come." When your time of favor comes, no one can stop it. When you have the favor of God, it lasts a lifetime. We need to pray as children of God, according to Luke2:52(NASB) "And Jesus kept increasing in wisdom and stature and in favor with God and men". When you have favor of God and men you are blessed with prosperity, mercy, kindness, and indulgence to mention a few of God's favor.

God Almighty will give us good understanding that give favor (Proverbs 13:15), and we will increase in favor with God and men.

Trust and obey

When you put your trust in the Lord, you will be fulfilled. Obedience to His words and direction is the best sacrifice, and it brings the fulfillment of God's will. As the old hymn says, "Trust and obey for there is no other way to be happy in Jesus, but to trust and obey." The Bible says in Exodus 19:5(NAS), "Now then, if you will indeed obey my voice and keep my covenant, then you shall be my own possession among all the people, for the earth is mine."

In the Bible, those who obeyed our God were fulfilled. The Bible says in Isaiah 1:19, "If you are willing and obedient, you will eat the best of the land." Our fathers Abraham and Isaac, to name just two, were blessed and highly favored because of their obedience. God blessed Abraham because he obeyed God's commands. In Genesis 22:17-18, I will surely bless you and make your descendants as numerous as the stars in the sky and as the sand on the seashore. Your descendants will take possession of the cities of their enemies, and through your offspring, all nations on earth will be blessed, because you have obeyed me."

Obedience leads to blessings as the Bible emphasis in Deuteronomy 28:1-6 If you will listen diligently to the voice of the Lord your God, being watchful to do all His commandments which I command you this day, the Lord your God will set you high above all the nations of the earth. And all these blessings shall come upon you and overtake you if you heed the voice of the Lord your God. Blessed shall you be in the city and blessed shall you be in the field. Blessed shall be the fruit of your body and the fruit of your ground and the fruit of your beasts, the increase of your cattle and the young of your flock. Blessed shall be your basket and your kneading trough.

Blessed shall you be when you come in and blessed shall you be when you go out".

What is God telling you to do? Are you obeying His voice and instruction? Obedience means having faith in God and trusting His Word and doing His Will. If you cannot trust God, you cannot obey Him. Obedience is better than sacrifice. Obedience brings your blessings.

This example shows the chains of events from obedience to blessing.

Obedience ➡ Faith ➡ Trust ➡ Blessing

Trust Him today and listen to His audible voice. Obey Him and let Him lead you on your path to success and happiness.

Speak the truth in love

Are you judging others or condemning them for their wrongdoings? Are you the person who crucifies others for what they do wrong? Are you difficult to approach and can easily detect the mistakes of others? Do you fight and argue when corrected, but are fast to correct others? The Bible says in Matthew 7:1-5(NIV), "Do not judge; or you too will be judged. For in the same way you judge others, you will be judged, and with the measure you use, it will be measured to you.

Why do you look at the speck of sawdust in your brother's eye and pay no attention to the plank in your own eyes? How can you say to your brother, 'Let me take the speck out of your own eye,' when all the time there is a plank in your own eye? You hypocrite, First take the plank out of your own eye, and then you will see clearly to remove the speck from your brother's eye".

We know people who do terrible things, have negative attitude, and speak ungodly things; these people are the ones who condemn others quickly for the wrongs they commit. The question is, do you speak and judge others in truth and love? Do you look at yourself first before condemning and gossiping about the wrongdoings of others? Do you look at the person in the mirror when a problem arises between you and your associate to detect the cause of the problem? How do your affiliates perceive the way you communicate about others?

We read in Peter 2:1(NIV), "THEREFORE, rid you of all malice, and all deceit, hypocrisy, envy, and slander of every kind. Like new-born babies, crave pure spiritual milk, so that by it, you may grow in your salvation, now that you have tasted the Lord is good".

Why did peter emphasize this? As a result of envy and malice, wicked people condemn others who are doing great and wonderful things. They also spread untrue stories about these innocent ones who are doing exploit for God in their community. Peter does not want us to be involved with malice, deceit hypocrisy and slander. He does not want us to spread negative stories about others and pretend to be godly when we know we are ungodly. Peter wants us to have the desire for spiritual assets and experience God's Goodness.

The Bible says in Ephesians 4:15(NASB), "But speaking the truth in love, we are to grow up in all aspects into Him who is the head even Christ." The Bible also informs us to say positive things about others. When your associates are doing the wrong thing, you can correct them biblically and tell them how God wants us to live in love. When you speak well of people, we are laying down the Godly example of how we want people to speak about us.

The Bible also emphasizes speaking well of others in Zechariah 8:16 (KJV): "These are the things that you shall do; speak ye every man the truth to his neighbor, execute the judgment of truth and peace in your gates." God will bless the words of our mouth as we speak in love and truth to those around us.

Are you still struggling with sin?

If you are still struggling with your sin, know that whoever controls the will controls the man. There are three things that can control your will and your actions, they are, *God, the devil, and yourself.* The devil knows he cannot take your will from you, but can only make you sin. That is why the devil tries to make you follow your own will in fulfilling the desires of your flesh and heart. In addition this is why you are still struggling with sin; you are still fighting with sins because you are doing things in your way and not the Lord's way.

The Bible says in Romans 7:15(NASB), "For what I am doing, I do not understand; for I am not practicing what I would like to do, but I am doing the very thing I hate." Stop struggling. There is an answer to this. All you need to do is break yourself loose by dedicating your life to fulfilling God's will. He already paid the price for your sins. Come, give your life to Him today and He will forgive your sins and promote you from where you are to marvelous glory.

Say this prayer: Jesus, forgive me my sins and renew a right spirit within me. I repent from my sin and receive you as my Lord and savior.

How did you receive your opportunity?

When opportunity comes your way, how did you receive it? Did you grab it honorably or ruthlessly? Did you recognize or ignore it. How did you treat those whom the Lord used as vessels of opportunity in your life? Did you honor them or discourage them? Your conduct in everyday life and your relationships with people are strong determinants of the opportunities that come your way.

There are categories of opportunity. As believers, we may categorize some as physical and others as long-suffering. Physical opportunities are those that come through relationships with other people; for example a person who honestly communicate with you on how to improve your life. A long—suffering opportunity takes you through a rough route which is painful and frustrating. Initially it requires more effort and time with no positive result; but at the end, it is an enduring success. Many people in the long suffering category lose the opportunity due to impatience and lack of endurance.

We meet different categories of people in character every day; we should use wisdom and understanding in dealing with these people. We also need patience, endurance, tolerance, and deep insight to understand them. Some may want to help you, but need to assess your personality before entrusting you with responsibility. It might be easy or frustrating. Do not easily fall into negative vibes you receive, but take the opportunities you can get from them. Remember, the way life is, the so-called frustrating man may be your God sent.

As a child of God, pray for wisdom to be able to deal with people, and maximize every opportunity that comes your way.

Opportunity is precious. Once lost, it may never be regained. God will give you the insight to recognize every opportunity in Jesus name.

Time waits for no one

You were born at a time set by God. The time was set for you to develop, attend school, obtain job, get married and have a family increase in age, and eventually be called home (die). How are you spending your time? Time is precious. It is like a chain of events, if you miss one event, it may be difficult to regain it. As the saying goes, "Time waits for no one." It is twenty-four hours a day, 365 days a year. You cannot determine or become aware of the time you will be called home (die).

We celebrate certain people in America today. During their time, they made history and made impartations that cannot be forgotten from generation to generation. How are you spending your own time? Are you helpful to your community, or are you self-centered? Are you encouraging or not? Do you include others in your schedule? Do you sacrifice your time to help others? What charitable organization have you considered to support with your wealth so that you will be remembered?

Life is not about you, but about what you make of it. If you look at your life, are you proud of your accomplishments, position in the family, community and among friends? If your answer is yes, congratulations! If your answer to the above question, is No? Can you do anything to correct the time you have lost, and now use your time effectively? Yes you can still receive help to regain the days you have lost because with God all things are possible.

Time is how you use it. Time is precious. Those who are called celebrities today maximized their time to get there. What about you? How have you used your time? The opportunity for change is now. As the Bible says in Corinthians 6:2(KJV), "Behold now is the acceptable time." The opportunity is open through our Lord Jesus to give you a new life of spending your time in life purposefully and achieved your heart desires.

How are you using your position?

You may say, "I worked so hard to get to this position of authority." It is great to acknowledge your new power of authority. But, my question is, how are you using the position? In every position, we find ourselves; we have to know that it is given to us by God. I am referring to positions given to you by God, not through other means. You have to know that you do not own your life, and the owner of your soul could come any time to get it without your awareness. What will you tell God about how you used your position?

Do you use your position to help or destroy? Do you use it to help others to succeed, or do you humiliate, frustrate, or punish honest workers? Do you victimize your good workers or fail to treat them professionally? Do you use your position as a boss or leader to follow haters' advice and punish honest individuals? I mean those who hate others and bring wrong reports to you to encourage you to dislike the innocent ones so that you can be used to ruin their lives. Look back and ask yourself if you have allowed yourself to be used by these deceitful colleagues, church members, or workers to hurt others.

When you find yourself in a group that believes the reports of fake friends and liars, you need God to forgive you for forcing innocent ones to resign from their employment and punishing them unjustly for false accusations. In Exodus 20:5, God says He will visit "the iniquity of the fathers upon the children unto the third and fourth generation of them that hate me." When you hate the innocent children of God working under you, you hate God and God's punishment will be upon you and your generations. Please resist being a ruthless boss and apply wisdom at all time so that you and your generations do not reap evil seed.

Let us look at this scenario, a staff member was relating her wickedness to a colleague she hated. She boasted about hurting people who have come along her path. For example at her daughter's school she made sure the school expelled the girl who fought her daughter. In addition she hated another woman that was her supervisor. She made the supervisor cried, made her life miserable and forced her to transfer to another office because she could no longer take the humiliating experience of this lower and wicked staff. Ironically, her colleague she was boasting to, did not realize that this boastful woman would subject her to the same wicked experience.

The boastful woman made the staff members, people in authority to conspire against the colleague she was boasting to about her wicked behavior. At work they started calling this innocent child of God names. The boastful woman made an attempt with the help of other supervisors, deputy directors, directors and labor union to punish the colleague (innocent child of God). She blocked her promotion, humiliated her and had the authority suspend her for false allegation. As a result of the allegation the innocent person had a heart attack. An ambulance was called and the life of the innocent colleague was saved. The boastful woman also made all effort to see that her colleague that was suspended did not get help. The boastful woman has strong connections with the union and has a brother on the police force. As a result this innocent child of God did not get any help but instead punishment through assignments of work, isolation and harassments. The boastful woman was power drunk and wicked. She was boasting to the colleague at the beginning of the scenario in order to prepare her for the heartless experience.

My question is why was she able to persecute her colleagues? She was able to prosecute her colleague because she acknowledges that some bosses allowed themselves to be used to do evil through hear says and what they want to believe.

Even though her colleague she was boasting to about her wicked ways experienced sufferings but God is greater than those sufferings. We read in proverbs 11:8(NIV) "The righteous person is rescued from trouble and it falls on the wicked instead".

As a boss listen to what people have to tell you and ask God to give you the spirit of discernment. Be wise in judging and using your power. Observe the people in your organization or company and their behaviors. Use wisdom in solving problems, Use questioning techniques for solution and also use your leadership to conduct conflict resolution among your staff. Do not encourage evil reports, storytelling, and lies against colleagues, among your staff members or church members, family members and friends in your community.

Some leaders in their leadership are not wicked but they are arrogant and disrespectful. There are some leaders who made themselves play the role of gods in their church, home, job and community. Proverbs 16:18(NIV) says" Pride goes before destruction, a haughty spirit before a fall".

Do you exhibit pride in your position and react harshly or ruthlessly? Are you drunk with power when you obtain administrative position? Do you look down on your staff? Do you regard yourself as a god?

Do you have pleasure in destroying other people as enumerated in the above story? In your home are you authoritative or cooperative spouse? Do you enjoy people worshiping you with insincere lip services? Are you heartless and vicious to your staff? The Book of Proverbs 11:7 (NASB) says, "When a wicked man dies, his expectation shall perish; and the hope of iniquity perishes".

You do not know what tomorrow entails; a servant today could become a boss in the future. Your impact on the people who come along your path counts, show kindness and be respectful to people despite your position of authority. Proverbs 22:8 (NASV) says, "He that sows iniquity shall reap calamity; and the rod of his wrath shall fail. As you climb up the ladder to become a leader, be kind to those you encounter on the way up, because you might need them in the future.

God is willing to change you and give you a heart that is full of love, kindness, peace, patience, and humility. God loves you and wants you to repent from your ways and turn to Him. According to Isaiah 55:7(NKJV), "Let the wicked forsake his way, and the unrighteous man his thoughts; Let him return to the Lord, And He will have mercy on him; And to our God, For He will abundantly pardon".

God is calling you, as a boss who is used to frustrating and making life miserable for people, to make a change to your behavior. Remember, that what you sow is what you reap. Choose today to start sowing good fruits. The Bible says in Psalms 103:3, "Who forgives all your iniquities". When you are willing to repent, God is willing to forgive you and accept you as his or her child; God loves you and He is happy to see you change from your wicked ways. As you start doing His will and obeying His commandments God will instruct and direct your ways.

You can pray this prayer with me if you are a leader or you have a vision of becoming a leader. I pray that the Almighty God will help me to be a God fearing, loving, dedicated and proactive boss. God help me to humble myself, and make you first in all my decisions. Please help me to treat my staff fairly; be a good listener and appreciate them. May God help me not to use my power and position to humiliate others but to be empowered by God's wisdom and understanding in Jesus name I pray.

Breakthroughs and excessive blessings

What is a breakthrough? A breakthrough takes you past a line of defense. It is an act or instance of breaking an obstruction. When you break through, you overcome an obstacle that is hindering your process, success, or promotion in life. Breakthrough is the restoration of what Satan has stolen.

The weapons for reaching breakthrough are praying, fasting, and faith with action. To break through, you have to acknowledge God as the source of your strength and be totally dependent on Him. God says to you "Get ready for my time of restorations!" The Bible says, in Joel 2:24-26, that God promised, and the floors shall be full of wheat, and the vats shall overflow with wine and oil. And I will restore to you the years the locust hath eaten, the cankerworm, and the caterpillar, and the Palmer worm, my great army which I sent among you. And you shall eat in plenty, and be satisfied, and praise the name of the lord your God; that hath dealt wondrously with you: and my people shall never be ashamed.

Jabez prayed the prayer of breakthrough when he said, "O that you would bless me indeed and enlarge my border, and that your hand might be with me, and that you will keep me from harm that it may not pain me." 1 Chronicles 4:10(NASB) When you need blessing, you must have the right attitude—that is, have faith that you can be blessed, and work hard to achieve your goals. Ask God to enlarge your coast and believe.

Lord, let thine hand be with me to bless and protect me. The Bible says in Ezekiel 34:26, "And I will make them and places round about my hill a blessing, and I will cause the shower to come down in his season; there shall be showers of blessings."

As we all know, blessing is from God and if He promised you no devil can change the promise. According to Genesis 12:2(KJV), "And I will make of you a great nation, and I will bless you, and make my name great, and thou shall be a blessing."

Ways to receive blessings:

Desire is not destiny. The decision you make positively to be blessed is of paramount importance and brought you where you are in life.

- Have a positive attitude, and have strong faith to face obstacles.
- Listen to the voice of the Holy Spirit for instruction, for example when God asked Abraham to leave his father's house so as to receive his blessings, He listen to the Holy Spirit.
- Discern your purpose for blessing; let your purpose be in a godly way.
- Get training or advice when necessary for improvement.
- Have expectation and believe in God for an increase.

The blessing of the Lord is upon you. We bless you in the name of the Lord. God will answer your heart's desires according to His plan for your life

Where can we find wisdom?

The Bible says in Job 28:12-28(NASB): "Where can wisdom be found? And where is the place for understanding? Man does not know its value, nor is it found in the land of the living. The deep says, "It is not with me," and the sea says, "It is not with me." Wisdom cannot be obtained from gold neither shall silver be weighted for the price. No measure of gold, silver, crystal, coral or pearls can equal it, or the price of wisdom is above rubies."

Then, where does wisdom come from? God is the only one that understands the way of wisdom, and He knows the place of wisdom. That is why we read in Job 36.5, "Behold God is mighty but does not despise any; He is mighty in strength and wisdom."

The source for wisdom can be found in these Bible passages:

- Job 28:28(KJV): "And unto man. He said, Behold the fear of the Lord is Wisdom, and to depart from evil is understanding."
- Psalm 51:6(NASB): "Behold, You desire truth in the innermost being, and in the hidden part you will make me know wisdom."
- Deuteronomy 4:6(KJV): "Keep Therefore, and do them [God's commandments] for this is wisdom and your understanding in the sight of the nations, which shall hear all the statutes, and say, surely this great nation is wise and understanding people."
- Proverbs 4:4-8(KJV): "He taught me also, and said unto me, let thine heart retain my words, keep my commandments and live. Get wisdom, get understanding, forget it not, neither decline from the words of your mouth."

Five ways to get and keep wisdom:

1. Fear of God.
2. Walk in truth, holiness, and righteousness.
3. Keep His statutes and commandments.
4. Retain His words in your heart and speak about His words.
5. Have a personal relationship with Him (prayer and fasting).

Wisdom is the principal thing. Therefore, get wisdom and with wisdom you understand. Wisdom is not about age. It can be given to anyone and everyone who seeks. It is a gift from God and cannot be inherited. The Bible says in Job 12:2, "No doubt, but you are the people; wisdom shall die with you". This means wisdom cannot be transferred. When God gives you wisdom, it is yours. Solomon could not give his wisdom to his children; his wisdom died with him. Wisdom can be found through prayer as Solomon did in King 3:7-12. He prayed to God and asked for wisdom.

Come and seek your own wisdom from God by asking him in prayer as Solomon did in the Bible. keep the above steps to retain wisdom.

Wisdom and fulfillment: What is the foundation of wisdom?

The foundation of wisdom is found through God. Man cannot give you wisdom, but God can. The Bible says in James 1:5 (NASB), "But if any of you lacks wisdom, let him ask of God, who gives to all generously and without reproach, and it will be given to him."

Wisdom is not automatic or neither is it an inheritance. It is not what you can claim as your birth rite. It is a gift you receive from God by asking for it. Wisdom of God reveals things that an ordinary man cannot know, but only God knows.

In order to get wisdom, you must first ask yourself and check your ways, to see if you lack wisdom. For example, what is your approach to life? How do you make decisions on issues and other areas where wisdom is necessary? Be truthful to yourself and acknowledge if you lack wisdom. The Bible says in James 1:6 (NASB), "But he must ask in faith without doubting, for the one who doubts are like the surf of the sea driven and tossed by the wind."

Wisdom is not about age. It is a gift that can be given to anyone regardless of the age. In the Bible, God gave Solomon wisdom at his age as a king when he asked for it: "Now, O Lord my God, You have made your servant in place of my father David, yet I am a child, I do not know how to go out or come in. Your servant is in the midst of your people who you have chosen, a great people who are too many to be numbered or counted. So give your servant an understanding heart to judge your people to discern between good and evil; for who is able to judge this people of yours" (1 Kings 3:7-12 (NIV). He asked and his request was answered by God.

In Daniel 2:19-22, Daniel went to God to ask Him to reveal the secrets in a dream. Daniel said; Let the name of God be blessed forever and ever. For wisdom and power belong to God.

How do you receive wisdom?

1. Pray and supplicate God.
2. Have a heart willing to receive.
3. Fear of God.
4. Walk in God's ways and keep His statues and commandments.

Ask God to give you wisdom with the fear of God, wisdom of ideas to propagate the work of God and ideas to prosper.

How can you increase spiritually?

As a child of God, who desires Spiritual increase? You must be willing and ready to do God's will. Isaiah 42:5 says, "And spirit to those who walk in it." How can you walk in it?

1. Study and meditate on the scriptures (reading your Bible daily).
2. Pray, fast, and praise God.
3. Walk in truth, holiness, and the fear of God.
4. Have the heart of love (the heart of God).
5. Have a personal or intimate relationship with God and allow the Holy Spirit to lead and direct you through God's instruction
6. Listen to God's voice attentively and submissively.
7. Commit your ways to God continuously and have faith in Him.

To increase spiritually you must be involved in the things of God. Your spiritual battery must be charged through spiritual activities such as joining choirs, evangelism, usher, Sunday school teacher, and prayer group to mention a few.

As children of God your spiritual life must be continuously recharged so that you can have power to resist the devil and take power over it. When Jesus Christ came out of the Jordan River, He was full of the Holy Spirit. Why? Because God Knew He will be tempted by Satan and also to spiritually prepare him for the works God had given Him to do.

As a child of God, to be increased spiritually means drawing strength from God because you cannot do anything by yourself but through God. We read in John 8:28, "I am He and do nothing on my own initiative, but I speak these things as the father taught me." Follow the teaching of our Lord Jesus Christ as He taught His disciples to pray and they will receive the power of the Holy Spirit (Praying in tongues). When you walk this path, God will show up to bless you spiritually as Act 2:17(NASB) says, "That I will pour forth My Spirit on all mankind."

In Ezekiel 36:27, the Bible says, "I will put my spirit within you and cause you to walk in my statutes and you will be careful to observe my ordinance." All God needs from you is obedience to His will and Word and He will increase you spiritually.

God I pray for spiritual increase to do your will and your work in Jesus' name.

The healing power of God

What are you going through physically, financially, emotionally, or in your spirit that seem impossible? I have good news for you, and it is the healing power of God. The Bible says in Jeremiah 17:14(KJV), "Heal me, O Lord and I shall be healed: save me, and I shall be saved".

For healing to manifest, you must have faith. According to Acts 14:9(KJV), ". . . Have faith you are healed." Your faith must be strong enough to override any negative doctor's report about your health. You must trust God for your healing. We read in Matthew 4:23(KJV), "Jesus went about healing all manners of sickness and all manners of disease among the people." Psalm 103:3 says, "God forgives all your sins; and heals your diseases." This is the confirmation from God's word concerning your sickness or issues of life that you are healed.

Over two thousand years ago, Jesus, our greatest physician, paid the price for us to be healed. As the Bible says Isaiah 53.5, "But He was wounded for our transgression; He was bruised for our iniquities; the chastisement of our peace was upon him; and with His stripes, we are healed." Jesus bore all our infirmities on the cross. All we need is to release our burden, sickness, hurts, and diseases to Jesus and let Him take control.

To have total healing through our Lord Jesus Christ, do the following:

1. Ask God for forgiveness (Psalms 51:1-4 and Matthew 6:12).
2. Walk in truth, holiness, and righteousness (Isaiah 58:8; Psalm 37:17).

3. Pray that you may be healed (James 5:16).
4. Have faith that you are healed (Act 14:9).
5. Proclaim the words of healing every day by faith (Isaiah 53:5, "with His stripe I am healed).
6. Plead the blood of Jesus on your health issue.
7. Give thanks to God for healing.

There is power in the blood of Jesus to heal your diseases. All you need is to acknowledge His power to heal you. As the Bible says in Isaiah 58:8, "Then your light will break forth like the dawn, and your healing will quickly appear; then your righteousness will go before you and the glory of the Lord will be your rear guard." When you put your trust in God and call Him for healing as we read in Jeremiah 33:3 (NASB) "Call to me and I will answer you, and I will tell you great and mighty things which you do not know." What you do not know is that God is the great healer. He has all the body parts for every area of your body that need healing in His possession. What you need is to ask Him through prayer and fasting for replacement, and you will receive your healing.

I pray that God Almighty will increase your faith to participate in the miracle work of His healing. You will have testimony to share when you believe, in Jesus name we pray.

Healing of finances

We are going through economic crisis all over the world. Some have jobs that do not meet their needs. Some are living a frustrated life because they continuously search for jobs. In order to survive, some people accept low paying jobs until they gain employment based on their qualifications.

Due to economic crisis some churches and ministries are struggling to have the necessary finances to meet their budgets some ministries and churches do fundraising activities to obtain money for their ministry. Why? Because of the unemployment rate among the church members, some members could not pay their tithes and offering to help the church with evangelism and the maintenance of the church.

God never intended a lack of finances to do the work He has called us to do. God does not want His children to be poor or lack good things in life. Now is the time for God to break the spirit of poverty, and release miracles of debt cancellation, and a flow of blessings into our lives, so that we may experience wealth and prosperity. The Bibles says in Psalm 112:3, "Wealth and riches shall be in his house; and his righteousness will endure forever."

God's promise to you is found in Isaiah 45:3(KJV): "And I will give thee the treasures of darkness, and the hidden riches of the secret places; that thou know that I, the Lord; which call you by name, am the God of Israel." God is aware of what you are going through and is ready to prosper you and improve your finances. According to Proverbs 22:4, "By humility and the fear of the Lord are riches, and honor and life." If you want your finances to be improved, you need to fear God in all your ways.

Ways to be financially healed:

1. Have faith in God's promise to meet your needs and mediate on the word.
2. Trust and depend on God as your only source, and have the fear of God in all your ways.
3. Pray and make your requests known to God (you know your situation).
4. Take away fear, anxiety, and worries, and focus on new Godly ideas that can bring you wealth.
5. Do not relent, but continually work hard, putting all necessary actions into place and depending on God for guidance.
6. Change old ways of thinking; be positive and believe that your financial situation can change with the help of God.
7. Honor God with whatever little you have, no matter your circumstances, and give Him thanks.

To be healed financially, you have to rely on God's supernatural supply and not on your own natural resources. The Bible tells a story in John 6:9(NASB), The disciples said, "There is a lad here who has five barley loaves and two fish, but what are these for so many people?" Jesus said, "Have the people sit down." Jesus took the five loaves and two fishes then He gave thanks. The food distributed to those seated. They ate, and had a leftover of twelve baskets that were gathered after they finished eating." God can heal your finances that seem so limited and increase them to meet your own needs. He can give you abundance so that you will be able to give more into the work of God and help others.

Here is a process of how God wants to heal your finances:

No Lack ➡ Divine Sufficiency ➡ Total Provision ➡ Continual supply

All you need is to put your faith in action and work hard. Let us pray this prayer together. O God bless me greatly and make me a blessing for others. May God bless you and heal your finances with continuous supply of His provision.

Healing of family problems

Many families are going through different issues in their homes. This is very unfortunate because as children of God, Jesus took care of our issues on the cross. They cannot share their problems with anyone but God. Some crisis arise over spouse, children, siblings, or parents. Some have allowed family problems to affect their focus and their health. Out of frustration some people have given up seeking the face of God through fasting and praying, because they did not get immediate solution from God. Some even said, they have tried different methods to seek the face of God on the issue but no positive result. Some have the feeling that despite their efforts in seeking the face of God the problems seem to increase and get worse instead of God's divine solution.

According to Job 1:7 (KJV), "Satan answered from the Lord from going to and fro in the earth and from walking up and down in it, Satan is looking for whom to devour." As children of God, we should recognize that Satan is there to destroy people's joy. We read in Ephesians 6:11(KJV) "Put on the whole armor of God that ye may be able to stand against the wiles of the devil."

As children of God, God has not planned for us to face our problems with our limited understanding and strength. God's plan for His children in every attack we experience is to be there for us and fight the enemy with his unlimited and unsurpassed power. According to Ephesians 6:10 (KJV), "finally my brethren, be strong in the Lord and in the power of His might." You must enter a spiritual union with Christ in which you become one with Him, not in your own strength.

The problems we might be going through could be a test of faith like the crisis Job went through in the Bible. We should not loose hope. Sometimes God wants to use crisis to get our attention and draw us closer to Him. As a result of this problem we become strong because our faith has been tested before we become triumphant.

God's desire for us is to stand firm, regardless of the circumstances. Satan might work on defeating us but God wants us to stand firm and believe that He is in the battle with us against Satan, because He loves us and will not allow us to face our crisis alone. According to the book of Job 13:15, "Who will be competent to say in the midst of their fiery trials, though you hurt me, yet will I trust in Him?" God wants us to go beyond our problems to a new level of spiritual growth. As you focus on God and have faith in Him, you will arise and occupy that new spiritual territory as Peter did when he walked on the water with Jesus, and Peter did not look at the storm again but called on Jesus for help, and he had victory (Matthew 14:30-31).

Paths to victory during trials:

- Recognize the works of Satan that he likes to destroy the joy of God's children (Satan's characteristic is to attack and destroy).
- Have an offensive plan to resist and fight against his attacks (using the Word of God).
- Your mind is the battlefield where the war against Satan must be fought and won. It could be won by not allowing fear, anxiety, or worries in your mind. Also, be optimistic and imagine victory with your spiritual eyes.
- Pray and fast so that Satan will not gain territory. You must constantly be on guard to rebuke the devil by the power of the Holy Spirit in you.
- Ask God to forgive you and your family of your sins, ask Him to help you live a truthful and righteous life.

- Do not doubt about your victory over Satan but believe in the powerful offensive weapon God provides to fight against Satan. Have faith like a mustard seed that victory will be yours.
- Recognize that the battle is not physical, but spiritual and must be won by the powerful spiritual weapon God has given you, which are the Word of God, Prayer, fasting and praising God, putting on the armor of God, faith, that victory is yours, no matter how serious the problems is.

Regardless of the problem you are facing, Satan will try to bring to your life series of issues to use in defeating you. God has provided victory for you. Even though you might have faced every trials, every circumstances, and every family problems, but be assured that:

- God's ultimate purpose is to support you.
- God is in control of all your circumstances.
- God has limitation on the circumstances Satan can bring to your life.
- With every circumstance that comes, God has provided total victory.

I pray that whatever situation you and your family are going through God will be there for you because you are not alone, God will show up and you will have victory.

Healing of the mind

Why are you still struggling with your thought and emotions? Why are you battling with your past hurts and memories? Why are you dwelling in self-pity, anger, and resentment? Why are you still having negative feelings?

We need to move out of the battlefield of our minds and resist the mental torture which Satan has inflicted on us. Jesus paid a great price for our release so that we can be totally freed, restored and redeemed. As a child of God who obtained salvation, you have the ability to receive or reject the thoughts that go on in your mind. You have the advantage over any thought that is trying to invade your mind and bring you to bondage.

Some of the thoughts that can put people into bondage are: unforgiveness, worries, hurts bad memories of the past, guilt, negative feelings and fear.

Recognize the fact that as you try to resist worry in the battlefield of your mind, the enemy will try to draw you back into an old way of worrying. You have to decide. Ask yourself the following questions, Do I want to stand against this satanic power of worries by allowing the Holy Spirit to take control of my thought or not? Unless the strongholds of worry and other undesirable states of the mind are dealt with, the Holy Spirit is severely limited on how He can restore your mind. He will never force you to get rid of your thought that you are unwilling to surrender.

You have to make the decision if you want to be set freed and be healed from worries. God's promise for you is in 2Timothy 1:7(KJV): "For God hath not given us the spirit of fear, but of power, and of love and sound mind." To have this sound mind you need to allow Christ to reign in your thoughts, and you need to have the mind of Christ according to 1 Corinthians 2:16(KJV). For who hath known the mind of the lord, that he may instruct him? But we have the mind of Christ. Those who have the mind of Christ have peace of mind.

Ways to heal the mind:

- Recognize what is causing the worries and see how it affects you. For example, issues of self, financial trouble, job worries, and family problems).
- Confess your hurts to God and ask Him to heal you of negative emotions.
- Ask God to help you forgive others involved, forgiving them as Christ forgives you (Colossians 3:13).
- Forgive yourself if you have any guilt and sinful emotions; confess and repent. Ask God to forgive your sins and heal your emotions.
- Release yourself from condemnation by an act of your will.
- Do not allow your mind to dwell in the past and remember old memories. When Satan tries to bring the past, refuse it.
- Refrain from vain imagination and negative thought; and educate your mind with the words of God.
- Encourage your spirit to overcome negative emotions. When Satan tries to remind you about feelings of anger, self-pity, resentment, etc., confess these feelings to God and take authority over them by the name of Jesus.
- Learn the power of praise and worship. When worries or negative emotions arise, begin to praise and worship God,

even if you don't feel like doing it. This will make Satan retreat, taking his band of attacks of worry away from you.

- Read and meditate on the word of God to teach you how to stand against the strongholds of Satan and receive your joy that adds no sorrow.

God Almighty will heal your emotions and give you the desires of your heart according to His will. When you seek the peace of mind as a child of God, He will give you a total deliverance.

Delay is not a denial

What have you been striving hard to get but time is dragging on, and it looks as if there will be no end? What desire is delayed so much that you have lost all hope, and the loss of hope has caused health issues, lack of focus, thinking and sadness? According to Job 39:12(NIV), "Can you trust Him; to bring in your grains and gather it to your threshing floor?"

I have good news for you: trusting Him as Abraham, Sarah, Hannah, Elizabeth, and Rachel did during their delays, which brought them great joy and honor, is not far from manifesting in your life too. When Job was going through trials, He still trusted God, and at the end, he gave glory to God. We read in Philippians 4:13(KJV), "I can do all things through Him that who strengthens me." Let God be your strength during this delaying period. In Psalm 37:4(NIV), "Delight yourself in the Lord; And He will give you the desires of your heart."

What exactly is the delay in your life? Is it a job, fruit of the womb, a financial Situation; a promotion, a health issue that is prolonged, family issues, a marriage issue, or something else? Whatever category you find yourself, God will make all the promises He has for you to come through. You need to believe in God and He will fulfill the desires of your heart and will never forget you.

I encourage you to take these steps of faith during your delay:

1. Ask God for forgiveness of sin.
2. Delight to do God's will.

3. Pray without ceasing, making your request known to God.
4. Fast, praise God, and give thanks to Him.
5. Have strong faith that cannot be moved.
6. Focus on the promises of God for your life (Hannah was focused in prayer).
7. Listen to the voice and direction of God (not to what people are saying).
8. See your blessings with your spiritual eyes, and don't focus on what is happening in your surroundings.

We read in Acts 17:26, "From one man he made every nation of men that they should inhabit the whole earth; and He determined the times set for them and the exact places where they should live." God's time to set you free from your delay is now because He will never deny His Children of great things. When it was Sarah's time, as the Bible says in Genesis 18:10(KJV), "He said, I will surely return to you at this time next year; and behold Sarah your wife will have a son." Sarah's delay was not a denial; she was made the mother of many nations (Isaac). Hannah's delay was not a denial; she became the mother of a great prophet of God (Samuel). Elizabeth's delay was not a denial; she became the mother of a great man of God that baptized our Lord Jesus Christ (John the Baptist). Rachael's delay was not a denial; she was the mother of the great dreamer (Joseph) who saved the people and the land of Egypt during famine.

How have you seen your delay? Do you see it with spiritual eyes, believing it is bringing your own greatness? The way you perceive your delay brings your blessing—if you count it all joy and continue to trust in God and obey Him during your delay. Your appointed time will come just as Sarah, Hannah, Elizabeth, and others received their visitations, and their stories changed.

God is not a liar. Whatever He says or promises He will perfect it, Whatever He has in His plan for you will be manifested and fulfilled. Delay is not a Denial.

Can God leave you?

If you do God's will, He will not leave you. Jesus said, "I know my sheep and my sheep know me." Jesus knows those who are His followers and obedient to His words, Jesus is a true friend of His followers, Jesus knows His friend and His friends know Him as well. They are aware of the nature of Jesus Christ, they know what He likes and dislikes. Jesus recognizes His followers because of their intimate relationship with Him. The followers of Jesus Christ understand and recognize Him as their Lord and savior. The true followers of Jesus Christ were never cast out.

Those who disobeyed and betrayed were rejected and abandoned For example Judas Iscariot, the disciple of Jesus betrayed Him therefore He was cast out. Saul, the king of Israel, was cast out at the end of his reign. Jesus said, "I am the way, the truth and the life; no one comes to the Father but by me." When you are not doing the will of God, He can cast you out, According to Jeremiah7:15(NASB), "I will cast you out of my sight. As I have cast out all your brothers; all the offspring of Ephraim."

If you have chosen your own way and refuse to change, read what the Bible says about the consequence of stubbornness. Isaiah 66:3-4 says, "They have chosen their own ways, and their soul delights in their abominations; so I also choose harsh treatment for them and will bring them what they dread. For when I called, no one answered. When I spoke no one listened. They do evil in my sight and choose what displeases me."

We have witnessed that God can leave disobedient and unyielding people. If we don't do God's will and refuse to follow His word, it is time to change from our disobedience and wicked ways. Let us return to God, walk in truth, holiness, righteousness, fear of God and establish a personal relationship with Him. God loves you. He wants you to repent of your sins, rather than Him leaving you. He is a God who gives people a second chance.

All He needs is your willingness to come back to Him; Then God will not leave you. God loves you, and that is why He said we should evangelize to win lost souls. Give your life to God today and He will be with you.

I want you to know that God is not a man that He should lie He will never leave or forsake you.

Why dwell on the past?

If you were asked to talk about your past, how would you describe it? Was it pleasant or bad? If your past was pleasant and you did not experience pain or suffering, I give God the glory on your behalf. If you have suffered in life, can you change your past or go back to it? If you answer is No, why are you still dwelling in the past? It is not the end of the world, there is still hope in Jesus Christ.

As the wise saying goes, "Do not let your past hold you down." The devil wants to do everything in his power to instigate your associate in bringing into your memory your painful past experiences. This is the devil's way; of making people unhappy, and have them develop the spirit of worry and fear. If you were in this category I encourage you to start a new life through our Lord Jesus Christ. Believe in Him and He will heal you emotionally and spiritually. In addition He will frustrate the individuals whom the devil are using to remind you of your past. Remember, Jesus came for sinners and not the righteous. He is willing to accept you if you could forget your past by accepting Him as your Lord and personal savior and follow His path and also do His will. You have to let go of your past and let Jesus be in charge.

The Bible says in Jeremiah 9:24(AMP), "But let him who glories glory in this: that he understands and knows me personally and practically, directly, discerning and recognizing my character, that I am the Lord, who practice loving kindness, judgment and righteousness on the earth, for in these things I delight, says the Lord." Choose today to delight in God and forget your past. Ask

God for forgiveness of whatever sins you have committed. Have a new start of your life and be happy in Jesus.

As the Bible says, old things have passed away, and everything in your character, behavior, focus, and love for God become new.

Say this prayer, Lord, I am willing and ready to forget my past and follow you. Save me Lord and use me for your glory.

God can demand relocation

Do you know God can demand relocation from us? We have seen from the Bible how God works by asking people to relocate to their miracle so that their blessing can be established. God asked father Abraham to leave his father's house in order to take him to the Promised Land.

When Jesus was born, Joseph was told to relocate to Egypt for the safety of the child Jesus when King Herod wanted to kill him. The Bible says in Matthew 2:13(KJV), "And when they were departed behold, the angel of the Lord appeared to Joseph in a dream saying Arise, and take the young child and his mother, and flee to Egypt, and be thou there until I bring the word: for Herod will seek the young child to destroy him."

When God wants you to relocate, obedience is required. The Bible says in Matthew 2:14(KJV), "When he arose, he took the young child and his mother by night, and departed into Egypt." Joseph was warned by an angel, and he knew by the gravity of the warning that he had to take the baby and the mother at night to protect them from the enemy.

Obedience is the key to walking in freedom and victory in order to reap God's promised blessing. God is not interested in, and will not accept an act of disobedience, and anyone who walks in disobedience cannot expect to reap God's blessings. The Bible says in 1 Samuel 15:22(NIV), "Does the Lord delight in burnt offering and sacrifices as much as in obeying the voice of the Lord? To obey is better than sacrifice, and to heed is better than the fat of rams."

In the Bible, God instructs many to relocate and to listen diligently with faith to His voice which led to bringing them blessings. If you were not where your blessing is designed to manifest for you, God can instruct you to relocate. On the other hand, if your enemies were too many, and your life is in danger, as we see during the birth of Jesus, God can request relocation for your safety and then direct you on when to return. According to Matthew 2:20 (KJV), "Arise, and take the young child and his mother and go into the land of Israel, for they are dead, which sought the young child's life." This means God had destroyed the enemy, and it was safe for them to return to Jerusalem.

Deuteronomy 11:27(KJV) says, "The blessing if you obey the commands of the Lord your God that I am giving you today." What is God telling you about the situation you are going through? We read in the bible that when God told someone to relocate, He did not use an intermediary for them; He spoke to them directly. If you were going through issues concerning your life, job, environment, or ministry and God is telling you to relocate or leave the place, obey God and follow his directions.

Do not be afraid or worried about what to eat or drink, because He will provide for you. When Joseph was told to relocate with Jesus and Mary, he did not think about it but he obeyed because of their safety. Here is a story about a woman who got a Job with the City of New York eleven years ago. This woman was very happy that she secured the job with the City. She loved the Job with the city of New York because she has to support the clients and meet their needs. She loves the job because it allowed her to have a positive professional relationship with the clients. She did not realize she would encounter a lot of problems with a colleague and the authority. The woman was attacked by the authority and a colleague in numerous situations. They collaborated with everyone in the organization. They blocked every step she made to improve her Job performance in order to receive promotion. They set up traps for her. They made several attempts on her life. They sprayed chemicals in the office, changed her seat to a secluded area in order to attack her. They tried to pour acid on her. While her enemies carried out all these dangerous efforts, God was saving this woman miraculously in the ways she could not explain. She would pray and fast for God's divine protection. But the problems increased as new employees began to try to destroy her at all cost.

In January 2009, God called her to leave the job. Her family did not agree with her; but she wrote the letter of resignation. Yet, her family took it and was not submitted. So the boss never received the letter of resignation. Her enemies did many things that threatened her life and she almost died in 2009; but God's miracles sustained her life. In September 2011, God called her again to leave the job. Then, her enemies assigned special clients to her who spread chemicals that made her dizzy and burned her throat. But, God sustained her again.

She did not leave the job. As a result the supervisor would give her many assignments. Even the supervisor from her native country was used to destroy her health by giving her excessive work. As a result of the excessive work her two hands were swollen, but God sustained her. When the attacks continued, God asked her to resign from the job, which she finally did in September 2012 without regrets. In this scenario this woman loved her job but the climate of the Organization and God's direction prevented her from keeping the Job. God loves her and was with her. God told her to leave the Job many times. She did not listen until she nearly died.

God can request our relocation or to leave a place for safety, as in the case of our Lord Jesus when He was born and also in the case of this woman who worked with the City of New York. When God instructs us to leave a place, we must do it without delay. Delay could cause death, disability or regret because delay is dangerous. In the above scenario, enemies almost killed the woman because she delayed with obeying God. However, God was greater than the enemies, and He is a merciful God for saving her life.

The Bible says in 1 Samuel 15:22(NIV), "But Samuel replied: "Does the Lord delight in burnt offering and sacrifices as much as in obeying the voice of the Lord? To obey is better than sacrifice."

Abraham obeyed immediately without telling Sarah. He was called the friend of God and received his blessing for his obedience.

Is God telling you to relocate and the fear of the unknown bothers you? Do not consider the opinions of your associate or anyone who can have influence on your decision. Listen to God and ask for His directions. He will provide for you and supply your needs as you obey and do His Will

I pray that God will give us the spirit of obedience.

How do you take correction?

Are you happy or angry when you are corrected? Do you take it as an expression of love from well-wishers or keep malice in your heart against them? I am referring to the godly way of correcting with love, not correction backed up by hatred, envy, jealousy and backbiting. How do you take it? Be sincere.

The Bible says in Proverbs 3:12(NIV), "For whom the Lord loves He corrects, even as a father the son of whom he delights." If the bible appreciates the importance of correction that shows us we should make correction as a part of our lives'. Change your attitude of pride when corrected in a godly way, and count it as all joy that the person delights in you to have corrected you. *Only good people can tell you the truth.* Correction allows others to let you see yourself, and taking it positively will change you.

We read in Jeremiah 10:24(NIV), "Correct me, Lord, but only with justice-not in your anger lest you reduce me to nothing". I will relate this passage particularly to a scenario. When we see our brothers and sisters doing the wrong things, we are not to correct them with anger or gossip that can be little them. We should correct them with the fear of God and the love of God in us. Let them see scripturally why the correction is necessary so that they can take it in good faith and it can influence them positively.

As children of God it is very important to take correction. It might be for your safety or to guide you in the right path. In Proverbs 5:10(NIV), "Stern disciple awaits him who leaves the path: he who hate correction will die". This passage illustration is that, if you have godly people correcting you and you failed to Yield, this could cause destruction. For example, someone that is always living a carefree life, drinking and smoking, partying and driving carelessly, this kind of person really needs to listen to correction in order to save his or her life.

Take correction joyfully and appreciate those God has sent to you, to sincerely correct you with love. In Proverbs 12:1, whoever loves discipline loves knowledge, but whoever hates correction is stupid. Spend time with the wise and be wise by taking correction. I pray that God will put good people that will correct you with the fear of God in your life.

Truth will set you free

Do you want freedom today from your sin? Are you willing and ready to be set free? If your answer is yes, the truth to freedom is Jesus. Developing a personal relationship with Jesus Christ is the only way to return to God. In John 14:6 (NIV), "Jesus answered, I am the way and the truth and the life. No one comes to the father except through me." We cannot earn forgiveness or salvation; rather, it is a gift offered to everyone through our Lord Jesus Christ. He said to those who believed Him, "If you continue in my word, then you are truly disciple of mine, and you will know the truth, and the truth will make you free" (John 8:32 (NASB).

To be forgiven and free from sin, you must admit you are on the wrong path and ready for a change. You must ask God to forgive your sins, and you must choose to turn to God's way. Do not fear that you've done something so terrible that God won't forgive you. I want to remind you that Jesus died on the cross to give you salvation. Jesus' death and His resurrection provide the only way to restore your relationship with God.

To receive salvation and eternal life, we must trust in Jesus' sacrifice for our sins and confess him as Lord (John 3:16(NIV), "For God so love the world that he gave his one and only son, that whosoever believes in him shall not perish but have eternal life." If you believe in him you will receive salvation.

When you ask Jesus to be your personal savior, you will receive the Holy Spirit. The Holy Spirit lives with the believer and gives power to live a Christian life. The Holy Spirit also provides strength to withstand trials and temptations.

Living a Christian life is to get rid of your old ways and invest in living a life of righteousness. For examples speaking in truth, fearing God in all your ways, worshiping God by attending services in Church, reading and meditating on the word and establish personal relationship with God.

If you declare today that you are turning away from sin, God Almighty will renew a right spirit within you, and you are set free in Jesus' name.

Say this with me: God, I confess my sins to you; forgive me of my sins. I confess you as my Lord and personal savior and need you to direct my life from today in Jesus Christ I pray.

God is Love

The Bible says in John 3:16, "For God so loved the world that he gave his only-begotten son, that whosoever believed in Him should not perish, but have everlasting life." God is love, and those who abide in love abide in God, and God abides in them. Whoever follows Him must obey His commandment that says, "Love your neighbor as yourself." The measure of love you have for your neighbor is the exact measure you get back from God.

God said He will love us freely. That was why He instructed us in 1 John 4:7(NASB), "Beloved, let us love one another, for love is from God; and everyone who loves is born of God and knows God. The Bible says in Psalm 145:20, "The Lord keeps all who love Him, but the wicked He destroyed." We love, because He, first, loved us, If anyone says I love God and hate his brother; he is a liar, for the one who does not love his brother whom he has seen, cannot love God whom he has not seen. And this commandment we have from *Him*, that the one who loves God should love his brother also. (1 John 4:19-20 (NASB)

How can you say you love God and have no feelings for people? An example of this is when people say they don't know how to give or help people. But, when they need help, they jump on others to help them. God does not want us to be selfish. We read in1 John 4:16(NASB), "We have come to know and believed the love which God has for us, God is love, and the one who abides in love abides in God, and God abides in Him.". If you are self-centered and think that the world revolves around you this is not God's way of showing love. If you are hateful, wicked and back slander you need a change of attitude because you have no love of God.

Have the heart of love instead than hatred. Love brings peace of mind, harmony, long life, positive thoughts, and good relationships. Therefore, walk in the love of God because God is love.

May God give you a heart of Love in Jesus name.

Deliver your heart

What is the intent of your heart? Is it of good or evil? An evil heart leads to hell, while a good heart leads to heaven. We read in Matthew 15:19(NIV) "For out of the heart come evil thoughts, murder, adultery, sexual immorality, theft, false testimony, slander. These are what makes a man 'unclean' but eating with unwashed hands does not make him 'unclean'" This Bible passage illustrate what an evil heart carries. Evil heart allows Satan to fill their heart to lie (Act 5:3). They are hearts that is not right before God (Act 8:21).

An evil heart cannot be hidden according to Proverbs 27:19(NIV), "As water reflects a face, so a man's heart reflects the man." If you have an evil heart and feel you can pretend to people otherwise, God sees your heart and know your thoughts and will reward you accordingly.

Let's refer to the Bible for the examples of those who did not deliver their hearts:

- Judas Iscariot had a heart that betrayed Jesus.
- Haman had a hateful heart towards Mordecai.
- Absalom, who was David's son, had a murderous heart.
- Jezebel had a heart of covetousness; his heart was to possess Naboth's possession.
- Ananias had a deceitful heart when he kept back some of the price of the land. All these men were destroyed because they did not deliver their heart.

God is asking you to repent according to Act 8:22(NIV) "Repent of this wickedness and pray to the Lord. Perhaps he will forgive you for having such a thought in your heart." God is a God of a second chance. He sent his son so that your sins can be forgiven and you can receive salvation. In Jeremiah 24:7(NIV), I will give them a heart to know me, that I am Lord. They will be my people, and I will be their God, for they will return to me with all their heart." The heart that returns to God is a good heart.

Pray to God to deliver you from an evil heart and renew a right spirit and heart within you.

Is God not good to you?

Did you count your blessings as you woke up this morning to see how great God is in your life, or are you focused only on what you are expecting from God or what you are going through presently?

Day by day we live by the grace and mercy of God. When you have life, there is hope that good opportunities can come your way. All you need is to trust in God, obey His instructions and have faith in His promises. Why not thank Him for what He did and what He will do.

As children of God, we should be thankful to God no matter the situation we find ourselves. We read in Psalms 100:4-5(NASB), "Enter into his gate with Thanksgiving, and into his courts with praise, Give thanks to Him, bless His name. For the Lord is good; His loving kindness is everlasting; and His faithfulness to all generation."

God is good to you because He made you in the likeness of Himself; He sustained our lives to this day. He gave us food, clothing, shelter, good health, jobs and our family. The psalmist says, in Psalms 95:2(NIV), "Let us come before him with thanksgiving and extol him with music and song."

I want to encourage you and inform you of the promises of God for you according to 2 Samuel 7:28 (NASB), "Now, O Lord God, You are God, and your words are truth, and you have promised this good things to your servant. This is a living word to prove that God has you in His plan to give you joy, blessing, favor, honor, grace, wisdom and anything you are asking from Him according to His will for you. I want you to take away that doubt and know that God is good all the time.

As a child of God; when you acknowledge that God is good in your life according to Proverbs 3:4, "Then you will win favor and a good name in the sight of God and Man."

Start today to appreciate God in your way of life and do not lean on your own understanding, but in God's understanding.

O Lord help me to appreciate you every day, count my blessings and be aware of how great you are to me. In Jesus name I prayed.

About the Author

Prophetess Oyetutu Osibajo was born and raised in a Christian home and family. She is the founder and pastor of Church of Light Evangelism Ministry (COLEM). This ministry was set up by the power of God for prophecy, prayer, healing, deliverance, and evangelism. She started her prophetic ministry at a very young age and had prophesied into many lives through the inspiration of God which has brought great testimonies.

Prophetess Osibajo was called by God to start COLEM with her prophetic ministry in 2008. At first she acted like Jonah in the Bible, running from God instead of starting the church. Even though she loved God and was still performing the prophetic work and helping other ministries, her obedience was partial. She paid heavy prices for her disobedience until she started the ministry officially in July 2011.

Prophetess Osibajo's life and experiences are proof that God can use anyone to proclaim His glory, even those who are condemned by people. As it is written in Matthew 21:42(KJV), "Jesus said to them, did you ever read the scripture, the stone which the builders rejected, the same has become the head of the corner stone; this is the Lord's doing, and it is marvelous in our eyes?"

She is a woman of truth and she proclaims the love of God. She helps and cares for people which exemplifies the focus of her ministerial life. As we read in 1 Samuel 16:7(NASB) "For man looks at the outward appearance, but the Lord looks at the heart."

Prophetess Osibajo's life is a living wonder and testimony to the work of God. The miracle power of God, which sustained the life of those whom, God has chosen to use to proclaim His glory.

CPSIA information can be obtained at www.ICGtesting.com
Printed in the USA
BVOW01s1429271013

334694BV00001B/101/P